NUBIA

ANCIENT KINGDOMS OF AFRICA

NUBIA

ANCIENT KINGDOMS OF AFRICA

JOYCE L. HAYNES

MUSEUM OF FINE ARTS, BOSTON

This book has been funded in part through generous grants
from the NYNEX Foundation and New England Telephone.

Second printing, 1994

ISBN 0-87846-362-3
© 1992 Museum of Fine Arts, Boston

Except where otherwise noted,
all photographs are by the
Museum of Fine Arts, Boston

Credits for illustrations appear on pages 63–64

Typeset in Syntax
Printed by Acme Printing Company,
Wilmington, Massachusetts
Designed by Carl Zahn and Peter Der Manuelian
Edited by Fredrica A. Harvey

CONTENTS

Foreword *by Rita E. Freed*   6

Introduction   7

Geography of Nubia: The Land and the River   10

The Peoples of Nubia   13

The History of Nubia   16

Kings and Queens of Nubia   25

Nubian Religion   33

Burials   40

Daily Life   44

Surviving Aspects of Nubian Cultures   53

Afterword
Nubia: A Black Legacy *by Edmund Barry Gaither*   58

Glossary   60

List of Illustrations and Credits   63

FOREWORD

With the opening of the Nubia gallery at the Museum of Fine Arts, Boston, in May 1992, unique and wonderful ancient African cultures will be available to the public for the first time in this country in a permanent and comprehensive installation. Realizing the significance of Nubia, Boston City Councilor David Scondras pointed to the need for an introductory guide to these cultures and offered to assist in its publication. This book is a result of his foresight and his challenge. It represents a cooperative effort on the part of an advisory committee set up to produce this work. The commitee consisted of Lorri Berenberg, Edmund Barry Gaither, Timothy Kendall, Peter Lacovara, Peter Der Manuelian, Yvonne Markowitz, Barbara Martin, Jan Michaels, David Scondras, and Theresa Young and myself. Lorri Berenberg, from the Museum of Fine Arts' Department of Education, chaired the committee. Joyce Haynes shouldered the main responsibility for its writing and organization, while Carl Zahn and Peter Der Manuelian were responsible for design and layout. Many others made valuable contributions to the manuscript, including: Timothy Kendall, Peter Lacovara, Yvonne Markowitz, and Sheila Shear, all from the Egyptian Department; and Edmund Barry Gaither, director and curator of the Museum of the National Center of Afro-American Artists. Valuable editorial advice came from Lorri Berenberg and Barbara Martin, Department of Education; Theresa Young, consultant to the Department of Education and director of the Kush Club; and Claudine Brown, deputy assistant secretary for museums, Smithsonian Institution. As editor, Fredrica A. Harvey was extremely helpful in the final stages. Also, many thanks are due to William J. Burback, director, Department of Education, for his tireless support and encouragement of this project. Janice Sorkow and the entire staff of the Photographic Services Department deserve much praise for providing the exemplary color and black-and-white illustrations for this publication.

Special thanks are due to Alan Shestack, director of the Museum of Fine Arts, Boston, for his constant encouragement of the establishment of the Nubian gallery and his advocacy of the present book; to Désirée Caldwell, assistant director–exhibitions, Museum of Fine Arts, for supporting this project and seeing it through the system; and to Carl Zahn, director of publications, and his staff, for adding this book to a busy schedule.

This publication has been funded in part through generous grants from the NYNEX Foundation and New England Telephone.

I hope that this brief introduction to the cultures of Nubia will provide as much joy to those learning about it as it has to those of us who have had the privilege of working on the Nubian collection.

Rita E. Freed
Curator, Department of Egyptian and Ancient Near Eastern Art

INTRODUCTION

The Museum of Fine Arts' Department of Egyptian and Ancient Near Eastern Art has explored and researched the cultures of ancient Nubia since the early part of this century. In 1906, George Andrew Reisner (fig. 1), head of the Harvard University–Boston Museum of Fine Arts Archaeological Expedition, was asked by the Egyptian government to head an archaeological survey of northern Nubia. This survey was necessary because plans were under way to enlarge the first Aswan Dam, which had been completed in 1902. Once the new dam was finished, the ancient remains of the cultures that existed between the First and Second cataracts of the Nile would be flooded and lost underwater.

Fig. 1. Portrait of George Andrew Reisner (1867–1942) taken in June 1938.

Soon after completing the survey, Reisner moved farther south, into the Sudan, to begin excavations of sites from later periods (about 2000 B.C.–A.D. 350). From 1913 to 1932, the Museum Expedition explored major sites, including:

- five massive mud-brick forts guarding the river at the Second Cataract
- the walled city and huge burial sites of the Kerma culture
- the royal cemeteries of el Kurru and Nuri (fig. 2)
- the Great Temple at the holy mountain at Jebel Barkal (pronounced Jeh-bell Bar-cal) at the Fourth Cataract
- the cemeteries of the city of Meroe (Mer-oh-ay).

The government of the Sudan agreed to award half of the objects found to the Harvard University–Boston Museum of Fine Arts Expedition, with the Sudanese choosing first what they would keep. As a result of these excavations, the Museum of Fine Arts, Boston, now houses the finest and most extensive collection of Nubian art outside of Khartoum. Highlights of the Boston collection include colossal sculptures of ancient Nubian kings, dazzling gold jewelry, one of the largest granite sarcophagi ever excavated, and ceramics of unequaled craftsmanship.

Reisner's chief excavator in the Sudan was Harvard graduate Dows Dunham (1890–1984). Dunham eventually succeeded Reisner as curator of the Museum's Egyptian Department, and published seven books and numerous articles on the Nubian excavations.

In 1986, Museum excavations in Nubia were renewed and have revealed new discoveries at the site of Jebel Barkal. The Museum continues to play an important part in the ongoing exploration of the history of Nubia. A timeline in figure 3 presents the major periods of Nubian cultures.

Thanks to worldwide interest in the fascinating cultures that make up Nubia's history, our knowledge of Nubia has increased greatly in the last decade. For the first time at the Museum of Fine Arts, Boston, this material is showcased in its own gallery. This installation provides a long-awaited opportunity to highlight Nubia's contributions to the ancient world.

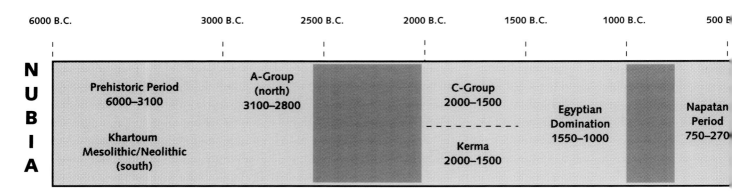

6000 B.C.		3000 B.C.	2500 B.C.	2000 B.C.	1500 B.C.	1000 B.C.	500 B

N U B I A

| Prehistoric Period 6000–3100 | A-Group (north) 3100–2800 | | C-Group 2000–1500 | | Egyptian Domination 1550–1000 | | Napatan Period 750–270 |
| Khartoum Mesolithic/Neolithic (south) | | | Kerma 2000–1500 | | | | |

Fig. 2. Sudanese workmen arrange shawabtis of King Taharka at the site of the pyramids of Nuri, Harvard University–Boston Museum of Fine Arts Archaeological Expedition, 1917.

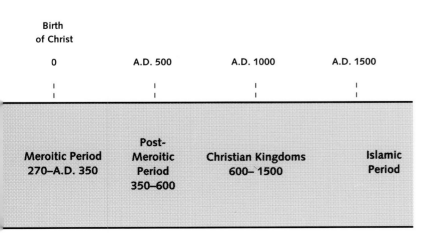

Birth of Christ

| 0 | A.D. 500 | A.D. 1000 | A.D. 1500 |

| Meroitic Period 270–A.D. 350 | Post-Meroitic Period 350–600 | Christian Kingdoms 600–1500 | Islamic Period |

Fig. 3. Timeline of Nubian cultures.

Uncertain.

GEOGRAPHY OF NUBIA:
THE LAND AND THE RIVER

Location   Where was ancient Nubia? If you look at the map of Africa and the Near East (fig. 4), you can see the modern-day countries of Egypt, the Sudan, and Ethiopia. To find ancient Nubia, go to Egypt, start in the north at Cairo, and follow the course of the Nile River southward. The northern border of ancient Nubia began approximately at the town of Aswan, in Egypt. Its southern border was near Khartoum, in the Sudan. (To learn more about the geography of Nubia, see the close-up map in figure 5.) Ancient Nubia was divided into two parts, Lower Nubia in the north and Upper Nubia in the south. The border between the two corresponds closely to the modern-day boundary between Egypt and the Sudan.

Nubia today is an ethnic and cultural area located in approximately the same region as ancient Nubia. Contemporary Nubians are an interesting cultural blend. They have much in common with the cultures in the interior of Africa and also have customs and traditions inherited from the Egyptian and Mediterranean peoples.

**The Aswan
High Dam**   In this century, the lives of the northern Nubian people were changed by the building of the Aswan High Dam (1960–1971). The dam, which was necessary for electrical power and irrigation for growing crops year-round, created floodwaters that threatened the heartland of the remains of the ancient Nubian civilization. Ultimately, much of Nubia between the First and Second cataracts was lost forever under the rising waters of the Nile, which formed Lake Nassar. Prior to the completion of the dam, the Nubians who lived in this area were moved into parts of Egypt and southern Nubia.

The River   In ancient times, people could not have lived in the desert areas of Egypt or Nubia without the waters of the Nile. It was a source of both water and food. The Nubians caught a variety of fish and hunted ducks and other waterfowl that lived along the river.

Farmers knew that every summer the heavy rains that fell in the Ethiopian mountains would flow down into the Nile, causing the river to flood its banks. Rich soil called silt was carried along by the floodwaters. When the river overflowed, the silt was deposited on the banks. The farmers used this fertile earth to grow lush fruits and vegetables in the desert climate.

From Aswan southward, the smooth flow of the Nile River is broken by large granite boulders, forming rapids called cataracts (fig. 6). In Nubia, six cataracts along the Nile make navigation difficult. Today, as in ancient times, boats have to be hauled out of the water and around the cataracts. This makes shipping hazardous, and sometimes impossible. It is often easier to travel overland than by water. The local people call the sixty-mile stretch of rapids between the Second and Third cataracts the Batn el Hagar, or the "Belly of Rocks."

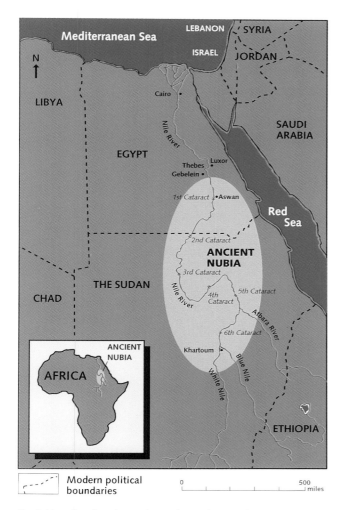

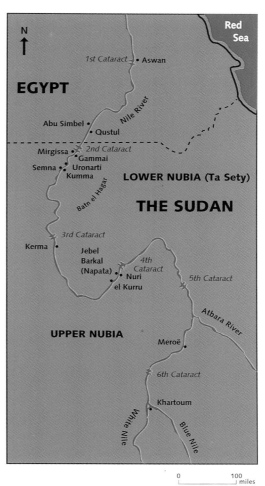

Fig. 4. Map of modern-day northeast Africa and surrounding countries, highlighting the location of ancient Nubia.

Fig. 5. Detailed map of ancient Nubia.

Landscape   Desert makes up 96 percent of all the land in Egypt and Nubia. In Egypt, the Nile is bordered on either side by a narrow band of rich soil, where fields of vegetables, fruit trees, and palms can grow. Beyond these strips of soil lie vast expanses of desert. Farther south in Nubia, the Nile also parts the desert landscape. However, farmable land is not as plentiful along the river in Nubia as it is in Egypt. In many places, the desert sands and granite mountains reach all the way down to the banks of the river. Therefore, little or nothing can grow, and the land for many miles may be uninhabited.

Because it does not rain in northern Nubia, the people had to live near the Nile for their water supply. As one moves south into Upper Nubia, rain does fall during the summer months. At that time and during the fall, the desert blossoms, and the plains are filled with grass. This climate

11

change allows the people who live in southern Nubia to spend part of the year farming and herding.

Gateway to Africa

For thousands of years and even today, Nubia's Nile Valley provided the only dependable way across the barrier of the great desert of Africa to the Mediterranean Sea. Exotic animals, skins, ostrich eggs and feathers, ivory, ebony, and most important, gold were brought from Nubia and other parts of Africa into Egypt and the Near East (fig. 7). Nubians exported some of these goods themselves. In other cases, they acted as commercial middlemen for Egyptians and charged taxes for these items, which they prized so highly.

Because Nubia was such an important and well-traveled trade route, it was known throughout the ancient world, particularly to the Egyptians, Greeks and Romans, and peoples of the Near East. It served as a cultural meeting place for travelers from the interior of Africa as well as from the Mediterranean world. The cultures of Nubia reflect a blend of the traditions of all of these people.

Fig. 6. Second Cataract of the Nile, with rocky Nubian landscape at Semna as viewed from the west bank of the river.

THE PEOPLES OF NUBIA

For thousands of years, many peoples have settled along the Nile River from the Mediterranean coast to the interior of Africa. As one moves from the north to the south, one would observe that the physical features of these Nile dwellers change gradually. The variations are barely noticeable from one village to the next. But, over longer distances, one can see differences in skin color, facial features, and height and hear several different languages. This is as true today as it was thousands of years ago.

The peoples of Nubia are an indigenous African population. They have occupied the middle portion of the Nile Valley since at least 6000 B.C. and likely for much longer. The Greeks and Romans called all the territory south of Egypt by the Greek name Ethiopia, which meant "Land of the Burnt Faces." This described its people, who had dark brown or black skin. Even the name Sudan is an Arabic translation of the Greek name meaning "(Land of the) Blacks." According to the latest studies, modern-day Nubians are most likely the direct descendants of the ancient Nubians.

The Nubians as Seen in Ancient Art

While both Egyptians and Nubians are indigenous African peoples, the ancient Egyptians represented themselves in their art differently from their southern neighbors. Egyptian artists used a red-brown paint for the skin color of Egyptian men, yellow for Egyptian women, and a dark brown or black for all Nubians. A painting from the tomb chamber of an Egyptian queen, in figure 8, shows her with black skin color, indicating that she was Nubian or of Nubian descent.

Characteristic clothing also distinguishes Nubians in Egyptian art. Notice, for example, the long, beaded Nubian belt in the painting of a Nubian soldier on his tomb stela (gravestone) in figure 9. Nubians can also be identified by their hairstyles. For example, figure 10 shows a procession of four different races of mankind. The Nubians have short, curly hairstyles distinctive from those of the Egyptians. Some Nubian men dyed their hair red and adorned it with ostrich feathers. This hairstyle is depicted in the Egyptian tomb paintings in figures 7 and 10.

Nubians painted or carved very few artistic representations of themselves during their early history. Therefore, Egyptian representations of Nubians, along with the remains from Nubian graves, are the best evidence of how Nubians looked prior to about 1000 B.C. However, starting about 720 B.C., Nubians created magnificent stone sculptures of their royal families. Two such colossal statues of Nubian kings in the Museum of Fine Arts, Boston, are fine examples of how they saw themselves and wished to be remembered. The two royal brothers Aspelta (Ah-spell-tah), in figure 11, and Anlamani (An-lah-mah-nee), in figure 12, appear like giants of men, standing in powerful, striding poses. Each is crowned with two cobras on his forehead and wears the tall, feathered royal Nubian headdress.

Fig. 7. Wall painting showing a procession of Nubian princes, carrying rings and bags of gold, arriving in Egypt; from the Theban tomb of Huy, who was the "King's Son of Kush" under Egyptian king Tutankhamun (1334–1325 B.C.).

Fig. 8. Kemsit, the Nubian queen of the Egyptian king Mentuhotep II (2061–2010 B.C.), and her servants; from a painting in her tomb chamber.

THE HISTORY OF NUBIA

Nubian civilization is among the oldest in the world. Most of what we know about the history of ancient Nubia comes from archaeology. It is apparent that the histories of Nubia and Egypt have always been intertwined. Both countries shared a past of conquering and being conquered by each other. When one country became weak, the other would dominate. Throughout history, however, the Nubian cultures retained their own distinctive characteristics, as evidenced in their symbols of kingship, art, costume, jewelry, hairstyles, pottery, dwellings, styles of burials, and gods, for example.

Fig. 9. Stela from Gebelein, Upper Egypt, of a Nubian soldier named Nenu (about 2100 B.C.), carrying a bow. The text states that he and his son are Nubian; both wear a traditional Nubian belt.

Prehistoric Nubia (6000–3100 B.C.)

In early prehistoric times, nomadic cattle herders occupied most of north Africa, including northern Nubia. In southern Nubia, a very different and highly advanced culture developed, known today as the Khartoum Mesolithic. Remains of this eight-thousand-year-old culture have been found near Khartoum, the modern-day capital of the Sudan. It was closely related to other ancient cultures spread across north and central Africa.

The Khartoum Mesolithic people subsisted primarily by hunting and fishing. Their pottery, perhaps the oldest known in the world, is sophisticated and advanced. Unlike the early civilizations of Asia and the Near East, in Nubia the establishment of settlements and the production of pottery seem to have occurred before agriculture began.

The Neolithic Period (5000–3100 B.C.) showed considerable advances in Nubian civilization. This culture began creating human figurines, slate palettes for grinding cosmetics, and Black-topped red pottery.

Fig. 10. The four branches of mankind according to the Egyptians, from left to right: Egyptians, western Asiatics, Nubians, and Libyans. From the tomb of Sety I (1291–1279 B.C.), in the Valley of the Kings, Luxor.

Figs. 11–12. Colossal statues of King Aspelta (left, 600–580 B.C.), and King Anlamani (right, 620–600 B.C), from Jebel Barkal.

The A-Group (about 3100–2800 B.C.)

By the beginning of the historic period (about 3100 B.C.), when the use of writing first appears in Egypt, ancient records tell us that independent kingdoms existed in both Egypt and Nubia. The Nubian state was centered in Lower (northern) Nubia. The Nubian name for this area is unknown, but the Egyptians called it Ta Sety, the "Land of the Bow," in reference to the famed Nubian archers. The archaeologists who first puzzled over the remains of these people did not know what to call them because their original name was unknown. In an effort to organize the materials from this culture, they selected the designation A-Group because this culture was the earliest group identified in Lower Nubia. Later cultures have been labeled B-Group and C-Group.

The rich graves of the A-Group kings contained gold jewelry, beautiful pottery, and stone vessels (fig. 13) that rivaled the wealth of the Egyptian kings. Many of these luxury objects were Near Eastern or Egyptian, indicating that the A-Group carried on extensive trade with those areas. In time, the Egyptian and Nubian kingdoms became enemies, and the Egyptian kings, the same ones who built the great pyramids, invaded Nubia. The Egyptians conquered the A-Group and ruled the "Land of the Bow" as a colony. However, south of the Third Cataract, beyond the area of Egyptian control, the Nubians remained independent and continued to grow strong.

The B-Group

Archaeologists gave the name B-Group to another phase of Nubian culture, which they believed followed the A-Group. However, little information on this culture exists. Currently, historians are in disagreement as to whether the B-Group has enough differences from the A-Group and C-Group to be called a separate group.

The C-Group (2000–1500 B.C.)

As with the A-Group, the original name of the C-Group has never been identified, because they used no writing. The C-Group existed in Lower Nubia from about 2000 to 1500 B.C. and lived peacefully side by side with the Egyptians. The Nubians farmed small, fertile areas along the riverbanks, raised cattle, traded with the Egyptians, and produced fine, artistic pottery (fig. 14).

Second Cataract Forts

About 1900 B.C., the Egyptian king Sesostris I, fearing the growing power of peoples farther south, began building a string of heavy fortresses along the Nile in the area of the Second Cataract in Lower Nubia (fig. 15). The massive forts were sophisticated structures, surrounded by enclosure walls that had fortified gates with drawbridges. Some had barracks and storerooms to accommodate up to one thousand troops. The forts also served an economic role, for they functioned as trading posts and collecting stations for the gold mined in the Nubian desert. The series of forts was designed so that the Egyptian troops manning them could signal each other. In this way, the forts could be used not only to monitor trade in Lower Nubia, but also to defend Egypt from the powerful Nubian

Fig. 13. A-Group (3100–2800 B.C.) pottery, jewelry, and cosmetic palettes.

kingdom to the south. Egyptian inscriptions tell us that the ancient local name of this southern kingdom was Kush.

The Pan-Grave Culture (2200–1700 B.C.)

A very different Nubian group that existed at about the same time as the C-Group was the so-called Pan-Grave culture. These people were named for their shallow, round graves, which looked like frying pans to the archaeologists. Some of the Pan-Grave people likely originated from the nomadic tribes of the desert east of the Nile, who were famed bowmen known as the Medjay (Meh-jay). Because the Pan-Grave men were skilled bowmen and warriors, the Egyptian kings hired them as soldiers and gave them lands in Egypt on which to live with their families (see the Pan-Grave bowman Nenu in figure 9). Pan-Grave settlements and burial grounds are found throughout Egypt and Lower Nubia. One of the few depictions of a Pan-Grave warrior is painted on the skull of a cow that came from a Pan-Grave burial (fig. 16).

The Kerma Culture (2000–1550 B.C.)

By about 1700 B.C., while the power of Egypt was declining, the great Nubian kingdom of Kush expanded its influence. It was centered south of the Third Cataract in a rich, fertile bend of the Nile. This Nubian group is known as the Kerma culture because the remains of its capital now lie within the modern Sudanese town of Kerma. Their kings ruled much of what is now the northern Sudan as well as parts of southern Egypt.

The Kerma kingdom became one of the most powerful states in the history of Nubia. The wealth of the Kerma kingdom is reflected in the extravagant royal burials of their kings (fig. 17). Kings were buried in splendor under huge mounds of earth the size of football fields. Inside special tomb chambers at the center of the mounds, the kings' bodies, unmummified,

Fig. 14. C-Group (2000–1500 B.C.) assemblage of human and animal figurines, pottery, a necklace, and an alabaster vessel.

Fig. 15. Drawing of fortress at Semna, Second Cataract (about 1900 B.C.).

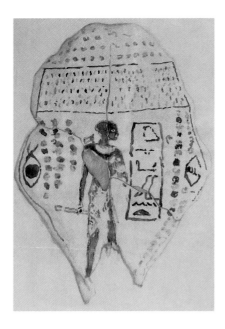

Fig. 16. Pan-Grave cow skull painted with the image of a Pan-Grave soldier (about 2000 B.C.).

were placed on gold-covered beds, surrounded by treasures of gold, ivory, and jewelry.

The Kerma kings formed an alliance with other kings from the eastern Mediterranean called the Hyksos (meaning "Rulers of the Foreign Lands"), who controlled northern Egypt. The Hyksos are best known for bringing horses and chariots to Egypt. By 1600 B.C., the Kerma people, together with the Hyksos, controlled most of southern and northern Egypt, while the Egyptian kings were ruling only a small district centered at Thebes.

Egypt in Nubia   The Egyptian kings from Thebes fought the Hyksos about 1550 B.C. and forced them out of northern Egypt. Then they turned their armies south and began a war against Kush which lasted about fifty years. Once

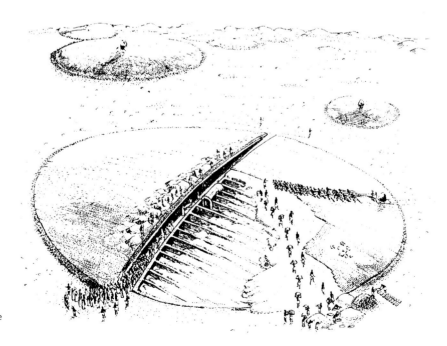

Fig. 17. Artist's reconstruction of a Kerma royal tumulus burial, showing a funerary procession entering the main corridor.

they destroyed Kerma, the capital city of Kush, then the rest of the kingdom fell, and the Egyptians gained control over all of Nubia as far south as the Fourth Cataract. In order to control the region, the Egyptians moved in their armies and reoccupied the Second Cataract forts in Nubia. Egyptian forces ruled Nubia as part of Egypt. A special office was created for governing this area led by a high-ranking Egyptian official known as the King's Son of Kush.

The Egyptians brought their administrators and priests into Nubia and built temples there. The Nubians began to worship Egyptian gods along with their own deities, and for more than four hundred years, Egypt ruled Nubia in this way.

The Kingdom of Kush: The Napatan Period (about 750–270 B.C.)

Centuries later, Egypt again became weak, while Kush became strong. In about 724 B.C., the Kushite king Piye (Pee-yeh), also known as Piankhy (meaning the "Living One"), conquered Egypt and declared himself pharaoh of all of Egypt and Nubia. He moved his capital to the great Egyptian city of Thebes. This began the Twenty-fifth Dynasty, the time when Egypt was ruled by the kings of Kush. The Kushites brought Egypt into their empire and governed it for about sixty years. They proved themselves to be impressive pharaohs, as they constructed many new monuments and encouraged a revival in both the literature and the arts in Egypt.

Their powerful rule came to an end, however, when Egypt was invaded by the Assyrians, who came from the area of modern-day Iraq. After destroying the combined Kushite and Egyptian armies about 660 B.C., the Assyrians forced the Kushite kings to flee back to their homeland, deep in Nubia.

The Kingdom of Kush: The Meroitic Period (about 270 B.C.– A.D. 350)

Far from the reach of enemy armies and unable to return to Egypt, the Kushites established a royal court in Meroe (fig. 18). The city of Meroe became the center of an empire that included not only much of Nubia, but also regions far south of modern-day Khartoum. Meroitic culture is strongly connected to central African traditions, while still making use of Egyptian styes and adding Graeco-Roman elements. Armies set forth from Meroe on annual campaigns to take control over surrounding peoples. Meroitic traders followed caravan routes east leading to the Red Sea and points beyond, or they went farther south, up the Blue Nile.

In this period, gods unique to Meroe, such as the lion-headed Apedemak (Ah-ped-eh-mack), have their own temples. Also, for the first time, the Meroitic people began to express their own language in an alphabetic script.

Meroe declined slowly in the third century A.D., perhaps because of too much competition for trade from its neighbors. During the fourth century, the culture seems to have mostly disappeared. In the sixth century A.D., missionaries from Egypt and Byzantium converted the various Nubian

Fig. 18. Meroitic pyramid and chapel relief (early second century B.C.).

peoples to Christianity. This remained their dominant religion until the fourteenth century A.D., when Islam came to Nubia.

Ancient References to Nubia

Since the Kushites spoke and wrote in the language called Meroitic, which has not yet been fully translated, most of their history is still unknown. What we do know of them comes primarily from archaeological remains and other ancient sources: the Egyptians, the biblical writers, the Greeks, and the Romans.

The Bible reports that Moses had a Kushite wife, and one ancient Jewish historian said that this wife was a member of the royal family at Meroe. Another legend added that the queen of Sheba was a descendant of the kings of Kush.

According to ancient historians, the kings of Kush were famous as great warriors. In the Bible, the prophet Isaiah spoke of Kush as a "land of whirring wings," probably because its armies, with their great leather shields, reminded him of a plague of locusts. The Greeks and Romans also put the Kushites in their legends because of their renown as warriors. In the story of the Trojan War, the Greeks wrote that a Kushite royal hero named Memnon fought on the side of Priam, king of Troy, against the Greeks.

The kings of Kush were known to be pious and devoted to their gods. Greek storytellers reported that Kush was a blessed place where the gods regularly went for dinner. The food offered there was said to be "the most pleasing to heaven."

The physical beauty and wealth of the Kushites inspired the ancient Greek writers. They called the Kushites "the tallest and handsomest" people in the whole world. One Greek fable reports that Alexander the Great, traveling in disguise, visited the court at Meroe and fell in love with its divinely beautiful queen. The same story tells us that the palace at Meroe was built on wheels and pulled about by elephants. The Greeks also wrote that at Meroe, people bathed in sweet-smelling fountains, buried their dead in crystal coffins, bound their prisoners in golden chains, and often lived to the age of 120 years. Although these stories are mythical, they reflect a sense of mystery and admiration that the Greeks and Romans felt for the ancient Nubians.

24

KINGS AND QUEENS OF NUBIA

We know very little about the beginnings of kingship in ancient Nubia. However, it is believed that the idea of "divine kingship," whereby the king rules as a god, came originally from central Africa. The concept eventually spread to the Egyptian pharaohs and then to the Roman Caesars.

As early as the A-Group culture (about 3100–2800 B.C.), we see graves of rich chiefs in Nubia as well as a cemetery of A-Group kings at Qustul (Cuh-stul), in Lower Nubia. These graves were filled with gold, jewelry, ivory, and hundreds of beautiful pots painted in imitation of baskets.

Further proof of the existence of Kushite rulers was found in the Egyptian forts in Nubia. From the forts, small, broken clay tablets were excavated which date to about 1900 B.C. On them were written the words "Kush" or "Ruler of Kush." The tablets had been deliberately smashed by the Egyptians. They believed that by breaking the tablets, they could magically destroy the might of their enemies. The powerful Kushite rulers were clearly a threat to Egypt.

The rulers of the Kerma culture (2000–1550 B.C.), possibly descendants of the A-Group, were buried in huge, earthen tombs. The size of their tumuli, or circular tombs, as well as their rich grave goods demonstrate the power and wealth of these early Kushite rulers.

In the eighth century B.C., we are introduced to the Nubian rulers by name. These kings were all members of a single royal family that rose to be powerful emperors of Egypt and Kush. They are remembered in history as Egypt's Twenty-fifth Dynasty (about 720–660 B.C.). Although they spoke their own language, they adopted the Egyptian language and writing and have left us a number of hieroglyphic inscriptions. These texts do more than record the kings' political accomplishments, as they also give us glimpses into their lives and personalities.

It was only through the royal women that Nubian rulers inherited the throne. All the kings and queens had to be born to a queen, usually the ruler's sister. They believed that their father was the god Amun. Therefore, they considered themselves to be part divine and part human.

Since there were many royal children eligible for the throne, the priests asked Amun to decide which ones would be rulers. In the coronation text of King Aspelta (see fig. 11), the king states that all his brothers were first led into the presence of the god, but none of them was chosen to be king. When Aspelta himself was taken before the statue of Amun, the god spoke to the assembled priests and dignitaries, saying: "This is the king, your Lord." After this, Aspelta was crowned. The priests believed that they could communicate directly with the god.

The ruler was required to do what the god Amun wished. Each was told how and when to wage war, make new temples, or restore old ones. The priests proclaimed this information. Therefore, every decision of the ruler was governed by the priests, who were the only ones believed to speak directly to Amun. Sometimes, the god even declared the moment that the ruler was to die. Then, the king or queen was expected to commit suicide. Most of them obeyed this command, but King Arkamani (Ar-kah-man-ee), who ruled about 270 to 260 B.C., did not. When he received this order, he marched with his army to the temple and killed the priests. Kushite history was no doubt full of rivalry and intrigue between the rulers and the priests.

Royal Symbols

The Kushite rulers wore special symbols of royalty, including some features from Egyptian dress, such as the royal kilt and certain kinds of crowns. But the Kushites had their own unique royal costume. Most typical of the symbols are the two rearing cobras, each called a *uraeus*, which they wore on their foreheads. The Egyptian pharaohs also wore a *uraeus*, but never more than one. Another feature of Kushite royalty is the cap crown. It is a skull cap, which fits around the ears and the back of the neck. Sometimes the cap has tall double feathers mounted on top of it, as we can see on the statue of King Aspelta (see fig. 11). Normally, it includes a headband, from which a pair of long, ribbonlike streamers hang down the wearer's back (fig. 19).

A gold necklace with ram-head pendants was also worn only by the Kushite rulers and can be seen on statues (fig. 20) and relief carvings. The ram has special significance because it was sacred to Amun.

Fig. 19. Relief carving of King Atlanersa (about 650 B.C.), wearing the double uraeus and traditional cap crown with headband and streamers.

Kings of Kush   The first of the great Kushite kings was Piye. The ancient records tell us that he swept down the Nile "raging like a panther" and conquered Egypt "like a cloudburst" about 724 B.C. For nearly sixty years, his family ruled Egypt and Nubia. They are credited with bringing Egypt out of a troubled time. The Kushite reverence for ancient traditions and the arts inspired them to restore the temples in Egypt and revive ancient religious ceremonies. They also copied and preserved ancient Egyptian books and supported a rebirth of the arts. The Kushites even built pyramids as their tombs in Nubia (fig. 21), just as the ancient Egyptian kings had done a thousand years earlier.

After Piye conquered Egypt, his reputation was very powerful. He was able to rule Egypt from the Kushite capital of Napata almost without ever having to set foot in Egypt. When a rebellion broke out in northern Egypt, the king sent his army to stop the rebels. The story of Piye's conquest of Egypt is recorded on a great stone stela at the temple of Amun at Jebel Barkal. This inscription gives us his view of the war and also some understanding of the king's personality. According to the text, he was extremely religious (fig. 22). He also appears to have been a king with compassion. The inscription tells us that he wished to avoid killing, if possible, and that he pardoned all his opponents in exchange for their promise to be loyal to him.

Piye's interest in horses is mentioned many times in his inscriptions. He personally scolded a conquered Egyptian prince who had allowed his horses to starve during the conflict. He also demanded horses as presents from the overthrown Egyptians. Scenes carved in the walls of the temple of Amun at Jebel Barkal show great stallions that were offered to him as gifts. When Piye died, in 716 B.C., he had eight of his best horses buried

Fig. 20. Detail of a bronze statuette of a king (possibly Taharka, 690–664 B.C.) wearing the classic Kushite necklace composed of three ram-headed pendants.

Fig. 21. The pyramids of Nuri.

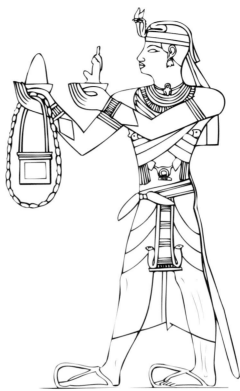

Fig. 22. Bronze offering stand of King Piye (747–716 B.C.).

Fig. 23. King Taharka (690–664 B.C.) offering a figure of Maat, a conical cake, a necklace, and a pectoral to the god Amun.

near his tomb in the royal cemetery. They were arranged in two groups of four, each probably representing a team for a four-horse chariot. The horses were beautifully adorned with ostrich plumes and colorful, beaded nets decorated with amulets of blue faience and silver.

The most outstanding member of the dynasty was Piye's son and third successor, Taharka (Ta-har-kah), who ruled from 690 to 664 B.C. (fig. 23). He is mentioned in the Bible as one of many powerful warring kings of the ancient world. No other Kushite ruler is named. An inscription tells us that he arranged for his mother to journey 1,200 miles from Nubia to Memphis, Egypt, so she could be present at his coronation. He wanted her to see him on the throne of Egypt. The text tells us that "She rejoiced exceedingly after beholding the beauty of His Majesty [Taharka]… crowned upon the throne of Upper and Lower Egypt."

Taharka's reign was prosperous; therefore, he was able to build and restore temples throughout Egypt and Nubia and to have many beautiful sculptures carved.

One interesting text tells us that Taharka's troops once ran a thirty-mile race across the desert. The race, longer than a marathon, took five hours. To avoid the extreme desert heat, the soldiers ran at night. The king followed along on horseback, and he found it so entertaining that he rewarded both the winners and the losers. The inscription tells us: "His majesty liked the 'contest' performed for him."

Taharka lost control of Egypt when the powerful troops of the king of Assyria invaded Egypt and defeated his army in 667 B.C. He then returned to Nubia, where he ruled until his death. An enormous pyramid marks his burial place at the cemetery at Nuri. In 1917, his tomb was excavated by the Museum of Fine Arts' Expedition. They found it had been badly plundered by robbers; however, more than a thousand stone shawabtis (sha-wab-ties), funerary statuettes, belonging to the king remained (some of these can be seen in figure 24), as well as many great treasures that were buried with him. Near the opening to the pyramid, the Museum archaeologists found something that the thieves likely dropped in their haste: a solid gold ring for an unusually large finger. Probably it had been worn by the great Taharka.

Fig. 24. Shawabtis of Taharka (690–664 B.C.) placed in his tomb in order that they might magically come to life in the next world and perform any hard labor asked of him.

One of the famous descendants of Taharka was his great-grandson Aspelta, who ruled from 600 to 580 B.C. His colossal statue is one of the treasures of the Museum of Fine Arts (see fig. 11). Part of Aspelta's fame is due to the rich grave goods found in his pyramid tomb at Nuri. Unlike many of the Nuri pyramids, Aspelta's was not completely robbed. The roof of the tomb had collapsed in ancient times, hiding the contents from thieves. Many fine works of art, as well as precious objects of gold, silver, and alabaster were buried within (fig. 25). A twelve-ton, granite sarcophagus of the king was also recovered from the tomb and brought back to Boston. These remains reveal that Aspelta was a powerful and wealthy ruler.

About 591 B.C., the Egyptians invaded Nubia, and Aspelta's armies were badly beaten. His new palace in Napata was burned to the ground, and he was forced to retreat south to Meroe. After this, Aspelta seems to

Fig. 25. Spouted, silver milk vessel, with gold and alabaster objects from the tombs of Kings Aspelta and Senkamenisken (sixth and seventh centuries B.C.).

disappear from history, as his final years of rule are not mentioned in the ancient hieroglyphic records.

Queens of Kush

Women held very high status in the Kushite culture (fig. 26). They played an important role in establishing who was going to be the next king or queen. Customarily, the throne was passed on from the ruler to a child of a sister. However, in some cases, one brother might be chosen to succeed another on the throne, as was the case with Kings Aspelta and Anlamani. Women could also be the rulers themselves, and many queens ruled the Kushite kingdom (fig. 27).

One well-known queen was Amanitore (Ah-mahn-ee-toh-ray), who lived about the time of Jesus (fig. 28). She was the daughter of a queen and ruled in her own right. Her husband appears with her in temple relief scenes. But we know that he was not considered a reigning king because he is never shown without her. Since she was a descendant of kings, and her husband probably was not, her pyramid was located in

Fig. 26. This gilt silver mask is an idealized image of the face of the Kushite queen Malakaye (Mala-kay-ah), early sixth century B.C.

a great royal cemetery along with other kings and queens of Meroe, and his was placed in an isolated, less important area.

Other important religious and government offices were handed down through maternal lines as well. Therefore, the "Mother of the King" and the "Sisters of the King" held very prominent positions in society. In fact, when the Kushites ruled Egypt during Dynasty Twenty-five, they placed the Theban area under the control of a royal Kushite princess. She was given the title "God's Wife of Amun." This was a powerful religious and administrative position, handed down from each Kushite princess to her successor. To receive this office, a woman had to be a virgin, because she was considered to be married to the god Amun.

Because of the significance of women, some classical writers incorrectly believed that Meroe was ruled *only* by women. One of the titles held by the Meroitic queens has continued in use as a name. Candace, meaning "Queen Mother" in Meroitic, is the origin of our female name Candace.

In many traditional societies, wealth and success are equated with a person's size. In Nubian cultures, women with full figures were considered models of prosperity. The Meroitic queens are usually shown as large, powerful women. They are covered with jewelry and wear elaborately fringed and tasseled robes (fig. 29). Their weight was symbolic of their life of wealth, power, and abundance and was considered the ideal form of beauty.

Fig. 27. This silver image of a goddess suckling a Kushite queen (eighth century B.C.) is a pose that is borrowed from Egyptian religious art. However, it is customarily the Egyptian king with the goddess and not a queen. This demonstrates the high status of the Kushite queens in their society.

Fig. 28. The powerful queen Amanitore (early first century A.D.) grasps the enemies of Nubia by their hair and holds a sword over them as she prepares to smite them.

Fig. 29. Queen Amanitore (early first century A.D.), in her finest garments, and her husband, King Natakamani, make offerings to the lion-god Apedemak.

NUBIAN RELIGION

Little is known about the religious beliefs of early Nubian cultures. Probably, very early Nubians identified certain sacred geographic areas and natural forces with their gods. What we know about their religion at that time comes primarily from an interpretation of objects found in their burial places. During the earliest period, archaeologists assume that Nubians, like Egyptians, believed in some form of an afterlife. However, because so few grave goods remain, we know little more than that. Because many of the cemeteries were used over long periods, we can assume that a similar religious system was shared by the A-Group and C-Group, as well as some of the later Nubian civilizations.

Shrines and small offerings to the gods lead us to believe that an informal religion existed, although no temples remain from this early period. Beginning about 2000 B.C., the Nubians established a shrine in a rock ledge at Toshka East, near the Second Cataract. Archaeologists have found hieroglyphic inscriptions as well as fragments of ceramics there that were deposited as offerings. These indicate to us that both Lower Nubians and Egyptians considered this a holy place. One inscription from about 1500 B.C. on the walls of the shrine reads: "An offering which the King gives to all the gods of Nubia."

Also, small clay figurines of animals and humans have been found in C-Group graves and at a C-Group settlement. Those found in the settlement may have been placed in a domestic shrine, or temple, as gifts or offerings to the gods.

The temples built in the Egyptian forts along the Nile at the Second Cataract seem to have been houses of worship for Nubians as well as for Egyptians. One can assume that Nubians living in the vicinity of the forts adopted some aspects of Egyptian religion. In fact, after the forts had been taken over by the Nubians, about 1640–1532 B.C., the king of Kerma sent for an Egyptian official to help rebuild the temple at the Buhen fort. This temple was dedicated to Horus, an Egyptian god.

The kings of Kerma also built their own temple (fig. 30), now called the Deffufa—modern-day Nubian for "mud-brick ruin." This temple was similar in plan to the small chapels associated with the large, round (tumulus) graves in the Kerma cemetery. However, the Deffufa was on a much grander scale. It measured more than 60 feet in height and was 150 feet long. It was surrounded by workshops, bakeries, and warehouses. This complex was decorated with columns, faience tiles, and a huge altar carved from quartz and covered with a blue glaze. The glazing of quartz was a uniquely Nubian technique. Numerous statues also decorated the temple. Some were made locally at Kerma, while others were imported from Egypt. This temple complex was as large or larger than any known of in Egypt at the time.

Nubians worshiped local deities as well as Egyptian gods. The ivory inlays found on the funerary beds in the great tombs at Kerma probably represented both. Fantastic creatures such as the winged giraffe may represent local deities. The Egyptian goddess Taweret (Tah-where-it), shown as a pregnant hippopotamus, also appears as an ivory inlay (fig. 31).

Fig. 30. The massive mud-brick temple complex of the upper Deffufa, at Kerma (about 1600 B.C.).

No doubt some of the Egyptian gods that were adopted into the Nubian religion were combined with local Nubian deities. For example, the ram god played an important role in Nubia. One can find statues of a ram-headed sphinx at Kerma, as well as burials containing elaborately decorated rams. This worship of the ram was well-established in Nubia before the cult of Amun arrived from Egypt. Very likely, the Nubians linked Amun to their ancient ram deity and considered him as their own. Many scholars believe that the ram connection to Amun originated in Nubia and was later brought to Egypt (fig. 32).

The cult of Amun was an important connection between the two cultures. The Egyptians believed that Amun was the creator and king of all the gods and the father of the Egyptian king. He was identified with the sun and the forces of nature. Egyptians represented Amun as a human or simply a ram. Nubians showed him in a unique way, as a ram-headed man. One can recognize Amun by his crown, decorated with a sun disk and two tall feathers (fig. 33).

Egyptian kings built colossal temples in Nubia during the period of their domination (1550–1000 B.C.). These temples became familiar features of

Fig. 31. Ivory inlays of the goddess Taweret and winged giraffes on a funerary bed from Kerma (2000–1550 B.C.).

Fig. 32. Nubian gold earring of ram head of Amun, crowned with double uraeus and sun disk, dating to the sixth century B.C. Enlarged.

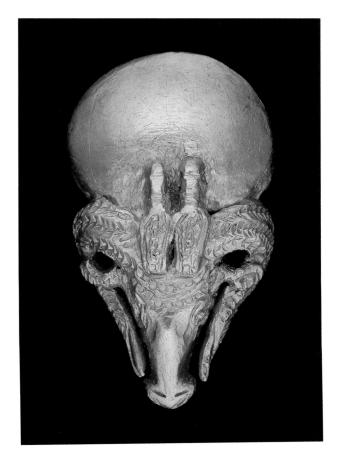

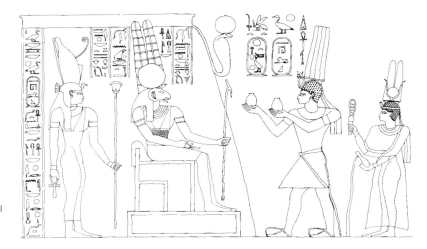

Fig. 33. Amun as a ram-headed man, seated within the sacred mountain at Jebel Barkal, from the reign of Taharka (690–664 B.C.).

the Nubian landscape. Two of the most famous are the temple of Ramesses II at Abu Simbel (fig. 34), built about 1250 B.C., and the temple of Amun at Jebel Barkal (fig. 35). The temple at Jebel Barkal was built at the town of Napata in about 1450 B.C. to mark the southern limit of Egypt's frontier. In size and importance, it rivaled Amun's main temple at Karnak, in Egypt. The Nubians maintained this temple, and over time, it became one of the most important religious centers in Nubia. A distinctive feature at this site was a small mountain, which the ancient Egyptians called the Pure Mountain. They believed that Amun resided behind its three-hundred-foot cliff and imagined him sitting there eternally on a throne (see fig. 33).

In front of the cliff rises a huge, freestanding pinnacle of rock (fig. 36). When Nubians and Egyptians viewed the mountain and pinnacle from

Fig. 34. Temple of Abu Simbel, constructed about 1250 B.C. by Ramesses II.

Fig. 35. Jebel Barkal with a computer reconstruction of the ancient temple complex.

Fig. 36. View of the pinnacle and ancient ruins of Jebel Barkal.

certain angles, they saw the silhouette of a head or crown with a cobra rising from its "brow." It was believed that Amun chose Jebel Barkal and the city of Napata to be the true center of kingship for all of Egypt and Nubia because of the cobra's importance as a royal symbol. Therefore, the kings of Napata believed themselves to be the true sons of Amun and the rightful heirs of the Egyptian pharaohs.

In the eighth century B.C., the powerful Kushite kings took control of Egypt. Believing themselves to be the legitimate rulers of Egypt, they successfully ruled the country for nearly sixty years.

Inscriptions tell us of some of the activities that occurred in the temple at Jebel Barkal. A statue of Amun in the temple was said to "speak" to the priests and even to proclaim who would be king. Each new king was crowned in the temple. Throughout his reign, the king was dictated to by the gods through the priests on matters of state and conduct of war. The temple of Amun was like a museum, for it was where all the crowns and scepters of the previous kings were kept.

Other temples at Jebel Barkal were dedicated to the well-known Egyptian goddesses Mut, Hathor, Tefnut, and a fourth whose name has been

Fig. 37. Gold jewelry image of the goddess Isis, with out-stretched wings, found in the tomb of a queen (late sixth century B.C.).

lost, probably Isis (fig. 37), who were honored as divine mothers. The goddesses were the protectors of the kings and the queens who are depicted in Nubian art suckling at the breasts of the goddesses (see fig. 27). Silver vessels for milk have been discovered in the royal tombs, and they bear inscriptions stating that drinking purified milk protected the ruler from all evil (see fig. 25).

Nubians worshiped other gods besides Amun. They identified their living kings with the god Horus, the legendary first king of Egypt, and their deceased kings with the god of the Underworld, Osiris. The ram-headed Khnum (Ka-num) was the deity of the Nile cataracts. Other gods were purely Nubian, such as the human-formed Dedun, god of the four directions (fig. 38). He was identified as the god of the land Ta Sety (Nubia) as early as 2300 B.C. in ancient Egyptian religious writings called the Pyramid Texts.

The supreme position of the god Amun at Jebel Barkal ends toward the close of the third century B.C. At that time, King Arkamani was said to have received an order from the god to commit suicide. But Arkamani, having a mind of his own, marched on the temple and killed the priests. With this event, the Kushites broke with their traditions. The royal burials, for example, subsequently were located much farther south, in Meroe. Egyptian was no longer the language used in inscriptions; Meroitic was used from then on. The Egyptian ideal went out of fashion, and kings and queens in art were represented according to new standards of beauty. Architecture, too, assumed many completely original aspects. The center of the kingdom shifted southward.

For the first time, temples were dedicated to a new "great god," named Apedemak, who came to have almost equal status with Amun. This god was represented as a powerful lion-headed man, often shown seated or standing on elephants or holding lions and elephants on leashes (fig. 39). On one of his temples, he appears fantastically, with three lion's heads and four arms and as a giant lion-headed serpent. By the first century A.D., the Egyptian goddess Isis seems to have become linked with him as mythical wife. Apedemak was revered as a protector of the king and state and as a god of war and victory.

Fig. 38. The Nubian god Dedun, seated on a throne
before the king Thutmose II (1518–1504 B.C.); relief
from Semna.

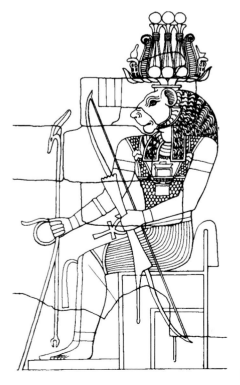

Fig. 39. The Nubian lion-god Apedemak, wearing
elaborate costume and crown, seated on a throne
(late third century B.C.).

Fig. 40. Khartoum Mesolithic sherds (about 6000 B.C.).

Why study burials? Archaeologists rely on the material remains in graves to tell them about both the religious life and the daily life of ancient peoples. When no written language is available, the objects must speak for themselves and provide a record of an ancient culture. The majority of the material remains of ancient Nubia and Egypt come from burials. Dwellings and the objects in them have often not survived. Rarely do people leave behind a house full of objects. In any event, the houses themselves have not lasted long since they were made primarily of impermanent materials such as mud, branches, and wood. Objects placed in graves are often the best preserved simply because burying protects them from natural elements and from robbery.

Certain categories of objects are customarily found in Nubian graves: jewelry, cosmetic implements, weapons, fine pottery. Items from daily life can be found throughout the entire spectrum of burials in ancient Nubia, from prehistoric times through the Meroitic Period.

The graves of the prehistoric and A-Group peoples were usually shallow oval pits. The body was placed on its side, curled up in a sleeping position, with knees drawn up. The greatest difference in the burials of these groups was in the types of grave goods.

The earliest objects placed in the graves were simple. They included primarily beads and other small ornaments made of stone, carnelian, bone, or shell. During the Khartoum Mesolithic period, the repertoire expanded to include pottery (fig. 40) as well as stone tools such as mace heads, adzes, and celts. The A-Group people, who came after the prehistoric cultures, were buried with more elaborate clothing and jewelry. Also interesting are the containers for storing food and drink, as well as vessels used for eating (see fig. 13) that have been found in A-Group burials. The placing of food and drink in the graves likely reveals that the A-Group had a belief in a spiritual life after death.

In some A-Group burials, a circular stone structure was built on top of the grave. This structure sometimes also had a small adjoining stone chapel area for receiving offerings. Pottery offerings and, occasionally, uninscribed stelae (gravestones) have been found in the chapels.

Some A-Group graves also included small human and animal figurines made of mud or clay. Because they were placed in graves, they likely had religious significance for the Nubians and were not just ornamental.

The circular grave form continues into the C-Group burials. They are well-known for the high, stone, circular structures, called tumuli, placed over the graves. The practice of having a burial marker on a grave was popular throughout Nubia at the time of the C-Group. Probably the stone tumuli were intended as memorials. The C-Group began a new practice of adding animal sacrifices to the graves. Skeletons of sheep, goats, cattle, gazelles, and dogs have been found in the same grave shafts as the human burials. Groups of cattle skulls are commonly found in some of the richest graves, suggesting that cattle represented wealth. Further, tall stelae, measuring up to six feet in height and positioned outside the graves, frequently were inscribed with pictures of cattle. Images of long-horned cattle also appear on pottery and in drawings on rock cliffs.

As mentioned earlier, the Pan-Grave culture got its name from their round graves shaped like frying pans. Their graves were located in both Egypt and Lower Nubia. Both the circular type of grave and the contents within firmly connect the Pan-Grave people to other Nubian cultures. This is evidenced by the classic leather kilts, the style of jewelry, and the horns of cattle, sheep, and gazelles that are found in the graves. One animal skull carries a unique depiction of a Pan-Grave chief with his name in hieroglyphs (see fig. 16).

In the Kerma culture, burial practices changed markedly. Graves of important individuals became more elaborate and large, and the burial goods were more numerous and lavish. Fine bronze objects in the graves indicate that the Kerma people were expert bronze workers. Kerma craftsmen are famed for their daggers (fig. 41), tools, and cosmetic implements. Jewelry was beautifully crafted from gold, silver, semiprecious stones, faience, ivory, glazed crystal, and shell.

The body could be buried in a variety of ways. In early Kerma burials, it was placed on a tanned ox hide, with another hide over it. Graves were small, with a tumulus superstructure. Sacrificed sheep are often found in the graves. Ostrich-feather disks decorated the heads of the sheep, and decorative horn protectors were placed on their horns (fig. 42).

Later, Kerma royal graves included enormous earth and gravel tumuli over the burial pit. A whole herd of cattle was sacrificed at each royal burial, and hundreds of their skulls were arranged around the rim of the earthen tomb. These tombs were for the rulers, whose unmummified bodies, frequently dressed in leather garments and wearing sandals and jewelry, were laid in a natural sleeping position on a bed. Their weapons were placed nearby.

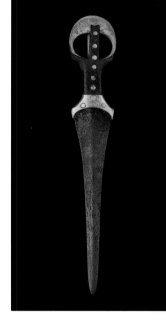

Fig. 41. Miniature dagger from Kerma dating to about 1700 B.C.

Fig. 42. Ram skulls with horn protectors, from a Kerma tomb (about 1600 B.C.).

41

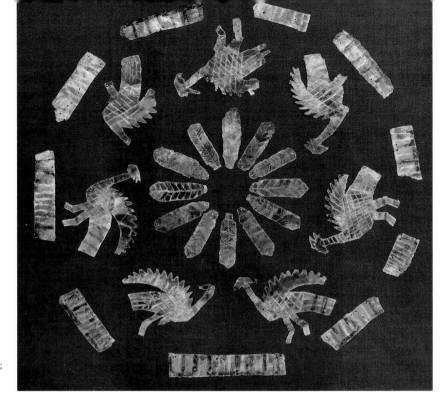

Fig. 43. Mica inlays in animal and bird images on leather caps; from the Kerma culture (2000–1550 B.C.).

Perhaps the most dramatic new element discovered in Kerma burials was their inclusion of human sacrifices. The bodies of finely dressed men, women, and children, possibly servants and wives, were found filling the corridors leading to the burial chambers of the royal tomb. Possibly these sacrifices were made so that the "servant" spirits could serve their ruler in the next world. The number of these sacrificed servants in a tomb increased as the Kerma culture developed and prospered. At the peak of this practice, hundreds of these sacrifices might be buried in a single tomb; one large grave contained some four hundred people. Some of the sacrificed figures wore leather caps with unusual mica animal and bird images attached (fig. 43).

In the eighth century B.C., when the Nubians ruled Egypt, a noticeable break with earlier Nubian funerary traditions occurs. During this period, we see the introduction in Nubia of many of the traditional Egyptian burial practices. For instance, Nubians began to build small stone pyramids for their rulers. The presence of canopic jars, the containers in which the internal organs were placed during mummification, indicates that the Nubians had begun mummifying their dead. In addition, the Egyptian tradition of including servant statuettes, or shawabtis, in the tomb became customary. At the same time, certain Nubian practices were discontinued. For example, human sacrifices were no longer included in the burials. The chief remaining connection to the earlier Nubian burial style was the funerary bed.

Burial practices became an interesting blend of Nubian and Egyptian customs after the location of the royal cemetery shifted south to Meroe about 270 B.C. Pyramids were still used for the burial of royalty (fig. 44).

Graves of high-ranking priests and dignitaries also had small, brick pyramid superstructures. As in Egypt, the body was still mummified and placed in an extended position in a wooden coffin. However, shawabtis were no longer used, and human servants once again were sacrificed and included in the burials. But, such sacrifice was on a much smaller scale than in the Kerma culture.

The graves of the Meroitic period also indicate Nubian participation in Graeco-Roman trade, as they contain large quantities of imported objects, including pottery, bronze work, glass, and silver from the Mediterranean world.

A unique Meroitic creation is a large statue of a human with bird wings (fig. 45). Most likely, this is an adaptation of the Egyptian ba bird, which represented a spiritual form of the deceased. The Nubian ba statues were set up outside the tombs of persons of high rank in Lower Nubia. Generally, all of these burial practices continued until Christianity came to Nubia in the sixth century A.D.

Fig. 44. Nineteenth-century view of the pyramids of Meroe (about 270 B.C.–A.D. 350).

Fig. 45. Reconstruction of a royal ba bird statue, Meroitic period (about third century A.D.).

Fig. 46. Pastoral scene showing men and women before a reed hut involved in the process of milking cows; engraved on a bronze bowl (second century A.D.).

DAILY LIFE

Dwellings Early Nubians occupied small and impermanent camps that they moved regularly. As hunters, fishers, and herders, they led seminomadic lives. They lived in tents made of cowhide or houses made of grass and reeds built on stone foundations. Traces of stone walls indicate that the later, C-Group people lived in open villages with more permanent houses. At Aniba (Ah-nee-ba), archaeologists have uncovered one-room houses as well as larger structures that were a cluster of several circular rooms. Both kinds of buildings had large, stone foundation slabs that were covered with mud and smaller stones. Wooden beams supported the ceilings.

Few ancient Nubian cities have been found. The largest was excavated at Kerma, around the lower Deffufa temple complex. Near the Deffufa is a large, circular building made of reeds and timber posts that may have been the palace of the Kerma king, since it resembles a modern African king's residence. Also found there were smaller versions of this type of building, as well as square ones made of mud brick. Some of the brick houses had porches or verandas. (This architectural feature was brought to America from Africa in Colonial times.) Both round and square houses were built throughout ancient Nubia (fig. 46) and can still be found in parts of Africa today. Depending on where they were located, houses were made from mud brick, stone blocks, or wood and reeds.

Livelihood Africans were the first to domesticate cattle. Nubians were primarily cattle herders. They also raised sheep and goats, and even made cattle drives across the Sahara. The climate in the Sahara at that early time was wetter than it is today, providing areas for grazing. Nubians made records of their travels and nomadic way of life in both rock carvings and paintings on rock walls. The rock representations depict animals and, occasionally, humans. They have been found all over the Sahara and beyond.

Because Nubia was rich in wild food that could be hunted, fished, or gathered, it was not until the Neolithic times, about 4000 B.C., that the early Nubians began growing grains. Wheat and barley were made into bread and beer, and dates and nuts were also cultivated. In addition, the Nubians traded with the Egyptians for a variety of other types of foods.

Lower Nubia was always important as a center for trade between Egypt and the rest of Africa. Raw materials from the interior of Africa, such as ebony, ivory, wild animal skins, and most important, gold, were traded down the Nile for food, jewelry, and other luxury items (fig. 47). Because of the wealth made by trading, a number of important cultures developed

44

in this area. This was particularly true during periods when the Egyptian control of the river traffic was weak.

Later, in Meroitic times, Nubia also became famous as a center for iron manufacture. In addition, Nubians used silver and bronze to create elaborate vessels, including copies of those that they had imported from Italy and Greece. Nubians traded these metal goods throughout the Roman world.

Nubians were famous as warriors, renowned for their strength and ability with the bow and arrow. This is demonstrated by one of the names for Nubia already mentioned, Ta Sety, the "Land of the Bow." Also as pointed out earlier, the Pan-Grave people were hired by Egyptians as mercenaries, and Nubian divisions were an important part of the Egyptian army. Soldiers from Nubia were also sought for armies as far away as Crete and Persia.

Writing   During the Meroitic Period (270 B.C.–A.D. 350), Nubians created their own unique writing system. Prior to this time, all known inscriptions had been in the Egyptian language. Meroitic texts of business documents, historical accounts, and religious prayers and offerings have been found. The religious inscriptions were placed on temple and tomb chapel walls as well as on funerary stelae and offering tables.

Fig. 47. Wall painting of Nubians carrying trade goods of ivory, ebony, and exotic animals; from the Theban tomb of Rekhmire (about 1450 B.C.).

Hieroglyph	Cursive	Phonetic value	Hieroglyph	Cursive	Phonetic value
𓃾	᎒	a	ᐳ	5	l
𓇌	5	e	◯	C	kh
𓀀	4	i	ᔦ	3	kh
𓃀	/	o	𖠋	3	sh
𓏭	///	y	□	V//	s (se)
𓏏	ᘐ	w	ᔓ	Ꮓ	k
𓃠	V	b	△	/3	q
⊕	ᗱ	p	ᗄ	5	t
𓂋	3	m	𐤟	/4	te
𓈖	ᖆ	n	◡	ꞈ	to
丰	Ⴟ	ne	𓂀	Ⴟ	d
.▢	ᜃ	r	⠇	,	word divider

Fig. 48. The Meroitic alphabet.

The Meroitic alphabet is composed of twenty-three symbols (fig. 48). The symbols were written in both a hieroglyphic and a shorthand, or cursive, form. Some of the signs were adapted from Egyptian hieroglyphs; however, the Meroitic language itself is much different from Egyptian.

Meroitic texts have been studied for more than a hundred years, yet a complete understanding of the language has still escaped scholars. Even though the sound value of each sign is known, the language itself has not been entirely deciphered. We still do not have a full understanding of either the grammar or the vocabulary. Meroitic writing remains one of the great ancient mysteries.

Jewelry Jewelry was an important aspect of adornment in ancient Nubia. Circlets, hair ornaments, necklaces, armlets, bracelets, finger rings, girdles, anklets, and beaded fabric were worn by both men and women. Even children were provided with an abundance of jeweled items. Earrings were probably introduced into Egypt by the Pan-Grave culture, although they were known in Mesopotamia from about 2500 B.C.

In prehistoric Nubia, organic materials such as shell and bone were used to manufacture beads, bangles, and pendants. Flint-drilled hard stones, colorful amulets, and beads of faience were popular with A-Group and C-Group peoples. In Kerma, clear quartz beads glazed a brilliant blue were strung as necklaces and sewn onto garments. The effect must have been dazzling under the bright sun.

Nubia was a rich source of raw materials for the ancient jeweler. Gold, carnelian, amethyst, and rock crystal were plentiful, and the art of metal-smithing was highly developed. Gold work from Napata and Meroe is among the finest in the ancient world. Meroe is particularly known for its enamel work (fig. 49), which includes several techniques, some experimental. The Museum of Fine Arts, Boston, houses a dazzling and extraordinary collection of royal jewelry consisting of beads, pendants (fig. 50), earrings, necklaces, armlets, bracelets, rings, and anklets. These objects of body adornment bring to life the images on temple walls. One can imagine the splendor of Queen Amanitore bedecked in an array of such jewelry (see figs. 28 and 29).

Clothing   Our knowledge of Nubian clothing comes chiefly from items found in graves. Nubians in the time of the A-Group and C-Group wore leather and linen loincloths, belts, and sandals. Leather caps have been found with the feathers that they wore in their hair.

The Kerma graves included items of leather, linen, and wool. Rich decoration can be seen on almost every item of clothing, embellished with pieces of mica or beads of faience, ostrich-egg shell, gold, or silver.

Leather seems to have been the most popular material for clothing. Nubians tanned the hides of sheep, goats, cattle, and gazelles to make caps, net coverings for the head, loincloths, skirts, girdles, and sandals. The caps, worn by men and women alike, were sometimes decorated with

Fig. 49. A hinged Meroitic bracelet of gold and bichrome enamel (first century B.C.). The goddess Hathor is seated in the central panel.

ornaments of mica cut in the shapes of animals, birds, and plants (see fig. 43). Men wore leather loincloths with frontal panels decorated with beads arranged in line patterns or diamond-shaped designs. Belts of leather or braided fiber, often decorated with beads, held the loincloth in place. Braided leather strips were also worn as girdles and used as sword belts.

Women usually wore knee-length leather skirts made from one or two large pieces of leather or from many narrow panels stitched together. The skirts were held in place by a drawstring, and this, too, was adorned with a variety of beads. Nubians embellished their leather skirts in many ways—stained red, pierced in patterns, or beaded with designs. Women also wore nets of very fine leather on their heads and leather tunics with fine seams and bead ornamentation. Footwear consisted of sandals made of thick cowhide soles with two loops that went around the toes. The sandals were held on with laces. Sandals, too, were ornamented, often with geometric designs cut into the soles.

Linen in fine and coarse weaves was found in most of the Kerma graves. Some pieces had decorative patterns of small, blue, faience ring beads strung onto the threads. It is unclear how Nubians used the linen, for no seams were found in it. Perhaps they wore it by wrapping or tying a single length of cloth around their bodies. In the Meroitic and Roman periods, Nubians also adorned themselves in finely embroidered woven garments made from high-quality cotton and silk imported from China.

Meroitic temple reliefs show elaborate styles of royal clothing. Queen Amanitore, at the temple at Naga, near the Sixth Cataract, is dressed in lavish robes ornamented with tassels and pleats (see figs. 28 and 29).

Furniture   Nubians, like Egyptians, used mostly "built-in" furniture made of mud brick that could be used as tables, chairs, or benches. The wealthy could afford beautiful furniture made of ebony wood decorated with ivory or even gold, such as the beds found at Kerma (fig. 51). They also made furniture out of basketry, as is still done in Ethiopia and other parts of Africa today. Colorful furnishings such as woven mats, trays, decorated wooden boxes, chests, and beds have also been found. Beds made today in Africa strongly resemble those made in ancient Nubia (fig. 52).

Pottery   Pottery is one of the most important remains that ancient people have left behind, because archaeologists can learn about and date ancient cultures by studying the pottery alone. Since different cultures created pottery in different shapes and styles, the pots can be used to identify specific groups of people. Ancient people continually altered the design of their pottery, ever so slightly. These changes, sometimes very subtle, can be traced through time. For example, a short-handled vessel might slowly evolve into a long-handled one. Once archaeologists can date the short-handled one as older, they can further interpret that the objects found with the short-handled pot are also older than the objects found with the

Fig. 50. One of the finest examples of Nubian craftsmanship is this pendant made of a rock-crystal base topped with a gold head of Hathor (eighth century B.C.). Enlarged.

Fig. 51. Bed with ivory inlays found in a royal Kerma burial (about 1600 B.C.).

Fig. 52. This contemporary bed of wood and palm fiber rope from the Sudan looks much like the ancient one (fig. 51) made nearly four thousand years earlier.

long-handled one. By the careful study of pottery, entire cultures can be identified and dated.

Pottery was used as dishes, storage containers, cooking pots, offering vases, and more. In dry climates such as Nubia's and Egypt's, ceramics do not easily disintegrate. Nearly every pot that was ever made has survived in some form or other and can be used for analysis.

Ancient Nubian pottery is renowned for its outstanding craftsmanship. It is superior in development, beauty, and creative design to any made by Nubia's neighbors. Nubians created their earliest pottery by hand, which makes the eggshell thinness and perfect shapes of their pots all the more impressive. They began to use a wheel to "throw" pots about 1500 B.C. but continued the handmade pottery tradition as well.

The earliest pottery known in Africa was made by Nubians in the area of modern-day Khartoum. It was produced by the Khartoum Mesolithic culture. Made of hand-shaped, unpainted, brown, fired clay, the pottery was elaborately decorated with punched and incised designs. The decorative patterns often involve combinations of dotted and continuous lines; thus, this type is called Dotted Wavy-Line pottery (see fig. 40). Archaeologists suggest that the Nubians may have used a catfish spine to incise, or carve, these designs. This type of decoration was used on ancient pottery throughout northern Africa and is still popular today in Africa.

Another Nubian ceramic type is Black-topped ware. These handmade, polished, red pots had a shiny black interior and rim. They were produced as early as the Prehistoric Period. No doubt it was the Nubians who brought this type of pot to predynastic Egypt. Some A-Group examples had a fine, rippled, burnished pattern on the surface (see fig. 13). The Black-topped tradition was taken to its greatest peak of development by the Kerma culture. The shallow bowls of the early Kerma civilization later developed into bell-shaped cups that are remarkably thin-walled and have flaring rims. These often have a distinctive gray band between the black mouth of the vessel and the red body caused by the extremely high temperatures under which these cups were fired (fig. 53). This style of pottery is still being made today in the Sudan.

Also characteristically Nubian are small, black C-Group vessels with incised lines filled in with white or colored pigments (see fig. 14). Examples of such vessels are noted especially for the endless variety of geometric line patterns. This decoration technique is also still popular on African ceramics.

The A-Group culture produced a unique type of pot: eggshell-thin, cone-shaped vessels painted with shades of red and orange iron oxide in intricate patterns that imitate basketry. This type is not found at any other time in Nubia.

The Pan-Grave culture also produced a distinctive decorated cup. It was of redware and had a finely combed or ridged surface.

Meroitic craftsmen also are renowned for their bowls, vases, and cups of extraordinarily thin ware made on the potter's wheel. This pottery is painted with red and brown designs and may also be marked with small, ornamental stamps (fig. 54). The lively motifs are a combination of Hellenistic designs and local patterns, such as lotuses, palm fronds, giraffes, crocodiles, gazelles, and frogs, as well as religious symbols such as the ankh (the Egyptian hieroglyph meaning "life").

Food   Nubians ate the meat of both domestic and wild animals, including cows, sheep, goats, pigs, hippos, gazelles, ostriches, geese, and ducks. The Nile was full of all kinds of fish that were caught and eaten, as were turtles. Bread and beer were staples, as were dates, figs, and nuts. Egyptian beer and wine jars have been found, suggesting that these imported drinks were popular. Very likely, the first imported beer was purchased in Nubia.

Pottery and baskets were used to store and serve food. Beautiful baskets were pictured in tomb paintings showing wares of Nubians (fig. 55). Today, Nubians still use baskets for serving food, and the colorful examples are popular items for sale in the markets (fig. 56).

Cosmetics   Oils and fats were used not only for cooking, but also as cosmetics. Both men and women applied eye paint, like the Egyptians. They wore it not only for beauty but also for its medicinal benefits, as it prevented eye infections. Palettes and stones for grinding the eye cosmetics have been found in Nubian graves, as well as toilet articles, such as mirrors, razors, and tweezers.

Fig. 53. Some of the most delicate and creative pottery vessels were made by the Kerma culture (2000–1550 B.C.).

Fig. 54. Meroitic vessel with lively painted crocodile-and-vine design (second century A.D.).

SURVIVING ASPECTS OF NUBIAN CULTURES

Nubians were among the most sophisticated and artistic peoples of the ancient world. Thanks to recent excavations and expanded interest in the history of Africa, we now are beginning to understand the everyday life of this ancient African civilization.

Many aspects of ancient Nubian cultures survive today, unchanged for more than thirty-five centuries, in southern Egypt, the Sudan, Ethiopia, and perhaps beyond. As previously mentioned, pottery very similar in decoration and manufacture to ancient types is still made and can be purchased in village markets of these countries. Today, Nubians create beds and stools in much the same way as those found in the graves at Kerma were made (see figs. 51 and 52). Even now, in remote parts of the eastern Sudan, people use wooden pillows similar to ancient headrests. Modern-day Nubians wear leather sandals identical to those found in ancient graves.

Nubians still commonly place square amulets, similar in shape to ancient Kushite and Egyptian types, around their necks for protection against disease and misfortune. Today, the amulets are small leather pouches containing folded papers with quotations that are often from the sacred Islamic texts of the Koran. Ancient Kushites adorned themselves with gold jewelry; modern-day Nubians continue the tradition. Likewise, some hairstyles have scarcely changed, as can be seen by comparing the ancient and modern methods of plaiting (figs. 57 and 58). Today, small children frequently have their heads shaved except for certain tufts, which are allowed to grow long, just as can be seen in ancient paintings.

Fig. 55. Wall painting showing
Nubian baskets containing
luxury goods in the Theban
tomb of Rekhmire (about
1450 B.C.).

Fig. 56. Basket shop in the suk,
or market, in Aswan (1984).

From the markings on small, pottery female figurines, we know that some of the C-Group women elaborately decorated their bodies with tattoos and patterns of scars. Many peoples of Nubia, the Sudan, and most of Equatorial Africa today continue the custom of adorning their faces with a series of distinctive permanent scars. Tattoos and scars may indicate social status or signify rites of passage. The arrangement of the scars varies from one group to another and may also serve as an identifying mark of one's tribal origin or affiliation. Many modern-day Sudanese wear facial scars identical to those that can be seen on Nubians represented in ancient Kushite, Egyptian, Greek, and Roman art (figs. 59 and 60).

One hallmark of both ancient and contemporary Nubian cattle herds is the presence of select oxen with artificially deformed horns. Today, these animals are seen primarily among the southern Sudanese, who keep them as pets and as objects of intense respect. Typically, the right horn grows naturally on these animals, while the left horn has been cut and forced to grow downward. Oxen with horns deformed in this way can be seen frequently in prehistoric Nubian rock drawings. Later, they appear in Egyptian art in scenes of Nubian war booty. Texts identify them as "oxen of the finest quality from Kush." In Kushite art, later still, the same types of cattle appear in scenes illustrating Kushite war spoils that have been taken from the southern tribes. The Kushites themselves are represented owning cattle with both horns symmetrically deformed—just like the animals of the modern-day Shilluk people, who are now centered along the White Nile south of Khartoum.

Many features of ancient Nubian burial customs have disappeared owing to the influences of centuries of exposure to the religions of ancient Egypt, Christianity, and Islam. However, a number of familiar features have remained remarkably unchanged. Although funerary beds are no longer placed in graves, Nubians are still carried on them in the procession to their graves. Nubians are no longer buried with grave goods; however, food and water jars are still left at the foot of the graves after burial. This allows relatives to make offerings to the spirit of the deceased as was done more than three thousand years ago in Kerma. Furthermore, both today and in ancient times, grave mounds are covered with a surface of hundreds, sometimes thousands, of smooth, white desert pebbles. The ancient meaning of these stones is not known; however, today each stone left on the grave represents a prayer that has been said for the deceased.

Another noteworthy characteristic of Nubian culture that has survived is the popularity of the sport of wrestling. In Egyptian art, Nubians are depicted as champion wrestlers and are frequently shown performing (fig. 61). Today, in the southern Sudan, among the people in the Nuba hills, wrestling is the primary sport of men. They gather annually to compete

Fig. 57. Plaited hair on mummy of Queen Nedjmet (1070–946 B.C.).

Fig. 58. Contemporary Sudanese girl with finely braided hairstyle much like the ancient plaits.

in great wrestling festivals. The winner becomes the man most likely to win a bride.

As mentioned previously, one ancient Kushite word that survives today is the female name Candace. It is actually derived from the royal title Candace, used for Kushite queens. The Greek and Roman explorers who visited Nubia carried back the incorrect report that Candace was the name given to all the queens of Kush rather than a title. The name Candace seems to have become especially popular after it appeared in the New Testament (Acts 17:27).

All of the features discussed above demonstrate the long-standing tradition upon which modern-day Nubian society is based. While many great civilizations have come and gone over the course of human history, the creativity, vitality, and individualism of ancient Nubian cultures survive and continue to flourish in our own age.

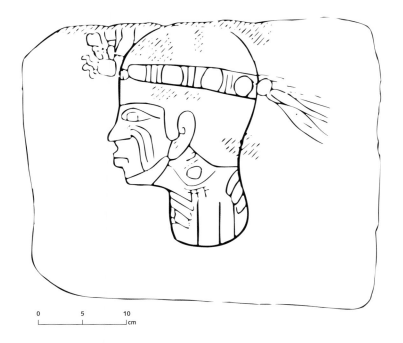

0 5 10 cm

Fig. 59. Ancient image of scarification from graffito of the first to second century A.D., from Meroe.

Fig. 60. Modern-day Sudanese girl with scarification on her face.

Fig. 61. Nubians wrestling, in a scene from the temple of Medinet Habu in Thebes, constructed by Ramesses III (1194–1163 B.C.).

NUBIA: A BLACK LEGACY

Afterword by Edmund Barry Gaither

American societies throughout this hemisphere have roots in cultures from many other parts of the world. For this reason, it is important to know about one another's past to better understand ourselves and others. Unfortunately, much of our knowledge of the past has been distorted by cultural bias and racial prejudices that we are only now beginning to correct.

As a consequence of slavery and its aftermath in the Americas, African history has not been fully or fairly presented. African-Americans and many others throughout the "New World" feel that Africa's contributions to history and culture have been devalued, misrepresented, or denied as a result. Examining Nubia will, therefore, help lead us toward an overdue reassessment of ancient Africa.

For Africans and their descendants throughout the Americas, the civilization of ancient Nubia is a symbolic legacy. They consider Nubia part of their own, broad heritage and view Africa as the source of their own, as well as many other, diverse cultures that have had wide impact globally.

Black people—whether Caribbean or North, Central, or South American—have preserved a profound consciousness of their African roots. Some still speak African languages; others observe a wide array of African and African-inspired religious, social, and cultural practices. Still others transform art, music, and dance through new, expressive forms created out of the synthesis of African and other traditions. In many places, political thought has been forcefully impacted by nationalist sentiments in which Africa figures prominently.

From the time of their arrival in the Americas, African-Americans have sought to strengthen their identity with Africa. In the United States in the sixties, the new identification took clear form in the cultural nationalism movement, at the center of which was the reclamation of ancient Egypt both as part of Africa and as the cradle of civilization.

Symbols from ancient Egypt were embraced by popular culture. Pyramids, images of pharaohs or their queens, and other similar designs proliferated. The most widespread was the Egyptian ankh, which appeared on necklaces and jewelry. Lectures and numerous other presentations reinterpreting the history of ancient Africa assumed increased importance and popularity.

Much of the discussion of ancient Egypt focused on the physical traits of early Egyptians. Frequently, these discussions did not distinguish between Egyptians and Nubians. In both cases, figurative works with facial features, hair textures, and styles associated with black people often occur. African-Americans could see aspects of themselves in ancient Nubian and Egyptian art.

Over the last three decades, important new perspectives on ancient Africa have emerged. These perspectives assert that Egyptian civilization was indebted to Africa to the south, including Nubia, for some of its formative ideas and that Egyptian civilization provided much of the foundation for Graeco-Roman civilization. Proceeding from this approach, Africa became not just the home of the earliest humans, but also the birthplace of civilization.

Inspired by an increased appreciation of early African heritage, many African-Americans adopted or gave to their children names such as Nefertiti or Candace. Others probed ancient texts, including *The Book of the Dead*, seeking to gain greater personal knowledge of Egypt and Kush.

Beyond this specific interest in Nubia and Egypt, African-Americans embraced Africa as a generalized ancestral legacy. Some changed their names to West African, Swahili, or Arabic. Because a growing number of African-Americans were becoming Muslims, Arabic names were especially frequent. Still others adopted the practice of wearing African or African-inspired garments. Ranging from *bubas* (dresses) to *geles* (head wraps), young blacks donned colorful outfits that proclaimed their awakening. A number of women, under the influence of the adage "black is beautiful," began to wear their hair in African-inspired coiffures, just as many men wore popular haircuts called Afros.

Greater knowledge of Nubia will enhance our understanding of black heritage while assisting in the restoration of Africa to her place in world cultural history. Additionally, it will inspire and challenge young people of African descent everywhere.

GLOSSARY

A-Group: comparatively advanced culture with trade, cattle raising, and possibly gold mining among the sources of their wealth; flourished about 3100–2800 B.C.

Abu Simbel: site of two temples created by Ramesses II about 1250 B.C.; located in northern Nubia near the Second Cataract area.

Amanitore: Meroitic queen who likely ruled in her own right; depicted in the temple of Naga.

Amulet: small religious object or figurine believed to provide magical protection for its wearer.

Amun: Egyptian god adopted by the Nubians and combined with their ram deity; depicted uniquely by the Nubians as a man with a ram's head.

Anlamani: king who reigned (620–600 B.C.) during the Napatan Period; his colossal stone sculpture is in the Museum of Fine Arts, Boston.

Apedemak: god in the form of a powerful lion-headed man often shown seated or standing on elephants and worshiped during the Meroitic Period (about 270 B.C.–A.D. 350).

Arkamani: king who reigned about 270–260 B.C., during the Meroitic Period; known from ancient texts to have slaughtered the ruling priests so he could control the kingdom as he desired.

Aspelta: king of Kush and Egypt who ruled about 600–580 B.C. His rich pyramid tomb at Nuri was discovered and excavated by the Museum of Fine Arts, Boston, in 1916.

Assyrians: ancient people who lived approximately in the area of modern-day Iraq and who forced the Nubians out of Egypt twice, in about 667 B.C. and again in 660 B.C.

B-Group: name of the culture thought to follow the A-Group, but whose existence is now disputed.

Ba bird statues: the ba was an aspect of the human personality, often translated "soul," which lived on after death. The ba was often represented in Nubia as a human figure with bird wings. From the second to third centuries A.D. in Nubia, ba statues were placed outside tombs.

Batn el Hagar: Arabic name meaning "Belly of Rocks," referring to the rocky rapids between the Second and Third cataracts.

Black-topped ware: some of the finest pottery ever made in the Nile Valley. The peak of production was achieved in the Kerma culture. It was handmade with a high, glossy, red polish and a black top, an effect created by the potters during firing.

C-Group: a seminomadic people who appeared in Lower Nubia about 2000–1500 B.C. Their camps were of reed or stone huts, and they had a cattle-based economy.

Candace: title of a queen meaning "Queen Mother" in Meroitic, which has come down to us as a female name.

Cataract: fierce rapids formed by granite boulders in the Nile. Six cataracts are located in the Nile starting in Aswan and extending south near Khartoum, in the Sudan.

Dedun: a Nubian god who takes a human form, called the god of the Four Directions.

Deffufa: a Nubian term for "large brick building." Also, the name given to the principal religious building at the site of the capital of the Kerma kingdom.

Ethiopia: a Greek term adopted by both the Greeks and the Romans to designate the land of Kush and surrounding areas. Derived from the Greek *aethiops* ("burnt-faced"), it meant "Land of the Burnt Faces."

Faience: type of porcelain-like ceramic made of crushed quartz, employed by Nubians and Egyptians primarily for small toilet articles, sculptures, and jewelry. The surface commonly has a blue, glassy glaze in imitation of turquoise.

Hieroglyphs: name given to the writing symbols used by the Egyptians. The script is composed of pictorial as well as phonetic symbols.

Jebel Barkal: site of the great temple complex dedicated to the god Amun located near the Fourth Cataract. The Pure Mountain, as it was called, was the most important religious center in Nubia.

Karnak: greatest temple complex in Egypt, dedicated to the god Amun.

Kerma: powerful Nubian kingdom, located near the Third Cataract, that existed between 2000 and 1550 B.C.

Khartoum Mesolithic: prehistoric culture from 6000 B.C. to 5000 B.C.; located at the site of the modern-day city of Khartoum.

Khnum: ram-headed god of the First Cataract.

el Kurru: site of one of the Napatan king's royal pyramid burial grounds.

Kush: Nubian name of a powerful kingdom. First mentioned in an inscription about 1900 B.C.; the name became standard for Nubia and was used by the Egyptians, Assyrians, and biblical writers.

Lower Nubia: northernmost part of Nubia, located between the First and Second cataracts.

Meroe: royal residence of Kush during the Meroitic Period, about 270 B.C.–A.D. 350.

Napata: northern capital and chief religious center of the kingdom of Kush. The Napatan kings were buried in pyramid tombs nearby at el Kurru and Nuri.

Nuri: royal cemetery of Napata, founded by King Taharka, who ruled from 690 to 664 B.C. The site contains the pyramid tombs of Taharka and nineteen of his successors and their queens.

Pan-Grave culture: famed bowmen and cattle herders who settled in northern Nubia and southern Egypt about 2200–1700 B.C. Archaeologists selected this name because of their distinctive pan-shaped graves.

Piye: Kushite king who in about 724 B.C. conquered Egypt and declared himself pharaoh of all of Egypt and Nubia.

Reisner, George A.: curator of the Museum of Fine Arts, Boston, and chief archaeologist for the Harvard University–Boston Museum of Fine Arts Expedition. He excavated numerous sites in Upper and Lower Nubia from 1906 to 1932.

Sarcophagus/sarcophagi: stone coffins in which royal rulers of Nubia were often buried.

Scarification: ritual application of scars on the body to indicate social status or to mark identification with a particular group.

Shawabti: statuette in mummiform shape usually made of stone or faience; placed in tombs to do manual labor on behalf of the deceased in the next world.

Stela/stelae: inscribed rectangular or rounded slab of wood or stone, carved and/or painted, serving as a funerary monument.

Taharka: greatest of all Kushite rulers of Egypt (690–664 B.C.), who, as Tihirka, is named twice in the Bible. His pyramid and rich grave goods, located in Nuri, were excavated by the Museum of Fine Arts, Boston.

Ta Sety: name given to Lower Nubia by the Egyptians, meaning "Land of the Bow," after the fact that the Nubians were formidable archers.

Taweret: popular Egyptian goddess in the form of a pregnant hippopotamus who is credited with watching over women in childbirth.

Thebes: capital city of Egypt from 1570 to 1070 B.C.

Tumulus/tumuli: circular burial mound used especially by the Kerma culture.

Upper Nubia: area south of the Second Cataract, extending to modern-day Khartoum.

Uraeus/uraei: most characteristic symbol of kingship, a rearing cobra worn on the forehead of Nubian and Egyptian pharaohs. Nubians were unique in wearing two cobras.

LIST OF ILLUSTRATIONS

All object numbers refer to Museum of Fine Arts numbers unless otherwise noted. All dates after royal names refer to the lengths of reigns.

Cover: detail of statue of King Senkamenisken (643–623 B.C.); from Jebel Barkal; granite; h. 1.47 m; Museum Expedition 23.731.

Frontispiece: detail of shawabti of King Taharka (690–664 B.C.); from Nuri; granite; h. 50.9 cm, w. 18 cm; Museum Expedition 20.227.

Fig. 1. George Andrew Reisner (1867–1942); photograph taken in June 1938 (expedition negative B 8968).

Fig. 2. Sudanese workmen arranging shawabtis of King Taharka with pyramids of Nuri in the background; March 19, 1917; photograph by G. A. Reisner (expedition negative D 335, E 7081).

Fig. 3. Timeline of Nubian cultures; drawing by Peter Der Manuelian.

Fig. 4. Map of modern-day northeast Africa and surrounding countries; drawing by Peter Der Manuelian.

Fig. 5. Detailed map of ancient Nubia; drawing by Peter Der Manuelian.

Fig. 6. Second Cataract of the Nile at Semna from the west bank; Nov. 6, 1928 (expedition negative A 4957).

Fig. 7. Wall painting from the Theban tomb of Huy, viceroy of Nubia under King Tutankhamun, Dynasty 18 (1334–1325 B.C.), showing the homage of Nubian princes. From N. de Garis Davies and A. Gardiner, *The Tomb of Huy* (London: Egypt Exploration Society, 1926), pl. 28.

Fig. 8. Kemsit, Nubian queen of King Mentuhotep II, Dynasty 11 (2061–2010 B.C.); from her tomb chamber wall; Metropolitan Museum of Art, New York; from E. Naville, *The XI Dynasty Temples at Deir el-Bahari* III (London: Egypt Exploration Fund, 1913), pl. 3.

Fig. 9. Stela of the Nubian soldier Nenu; from Gebelein, Dynasty 9–10 (2213–2035 B.C.); painted sandstone; l. 45 cm, h. 37 cm; purchased by A. M. Lythgoe, 03.1848.

Fig. 10. The four branches of mankind (Egyptians, western Asiatics, Nubians, and Libyans); from the tomb of King Sety I, Dynasty 19 (1291–1279 B.C.); Hall E; left side; Book of Gates, Fourth Division; photograph from K. Lepsius, *Denkmaeler aus Aegypten und Aethiopien…* (Berlin: Nicolaische Buchhandlung, 1842–45), Abt. 3, pl. 136.

Fig. 11. Colossal statue of King Aspelta (600–580 B.C.); from the temple of Amun at Jebel Barkal; granite; h. 3.32 m; Museum Expedition 23.730.

Fig. 12. Colossal statue of King Anlamani (620–600 B.C.); from the temple of Amun Jebel Barkal; granite; h. about 3.81 m; Museum Expedition 23.732.

Fig. 13. Assemblage of A-Group objects: three bowls, bracelet, two of a set of four bracelets, mirror, palette, diamond-shaped palette, necklace; 3100–2800 B.C.; ceramic, stone, shell, mica, and quartz; gift of G. A. Reisner, and Emily Esther Sears Fund, 03.1613, 19.1539, 19.1543, 98/806, no. #, 137/10, 137/4/11, 137/3/10, no #.

Fig. 14. Assemblage of C-Group objects (2000–1500 B.C.); from Lower Nubia; ceramic, alabaster (calcite), carnelian, and faience; gift of G. A. Reisner and G. Steindorff; human figurine, no #: h. 11.3 cm, max. w. 8.5 cm; animal figurine, 40/114/P: h. 10 cm, l. 12 cm; cup, 101/151/1: h. 9 cm, diam. 12.5 cm; cup, 101/80/6:

h. 8.2 cm, diam. 12.7 cm; large Black-topped bowl, 101/424/6: h. 13 cm, diam. 22.5 cm; kohl pot and lid, 69/61/3 (pot) and 58/119/2 (lid): h. with lid 5.2 cm; bead necklace, no #: l. 94 cm.

Fig. 15. Drawing of fortress at Semna; painting by Alan Sorrell (1957); courtesy Trustees of the British Museum.

Fig. 16. Pan-Grave cow skull painted with the image of a Pan-Grave warrior; British Museum 3252, watercolor copy by Nicholas Thayer, after G. Brunton, *Mostagedda and the Tasian Culture* (London: Bernard Quaritch, 1937), pl. 76.

Fig. 17. Large Kerma royal tumulus burial; from David O'Connor, "Ancient Egypt and Black Africa—Early Contacts," *Expedition* 14 (1971), p. 7, fig. 3.

Fig. 18. View of Meroitic chapel relief and pyramid; Beg. N. 13, King Nakyrinsan (early second century B.C.); photograph by Timothy Kendall.

Fig. 19. The front of the barque stand of King Atlanersa (about 650 B.C.); from Jebel Barkal; granite; h. 117 cm, w. 152 cm, d. 152 cm; Museum Expedition 23.728; drawing by Peter Der Manuelian.

Fig. 20. Statue of an unknown Nubian king (possibly Taharka, sixth century B.C.); from the temple of Amun Jebel Barkal; bronze with traces of gilding on crown; h. 19.9 cm, w. 8.5 cm, thickness 7.5 cm; Museum Expedition 21.3096.

Fig. 21. Pyramids at Nuri; photograph by Timothy Kendall.

Fig. 22. Offering stand of King Piye (747–716 B.C.); from el Kurru; bronze; h. 81.1 cm, diam. 45 cm; Museum Expedition 21.3238.

Fig. 23. King Taharka presenting offerings; from the hypostyle hall of temple T at Kawa (about 680 B.C.); redrawn by Nicholas Thayer and Peter Der Manuelian.

Fig. 24. Shawabtis of King Taharka (690–664 B.C.); from Nuri; alabaster (calcite), granite, and steatite; h. 10–35 cm; Museum Expedition.

Fig. 25. Ritual objects of Kings Senkamenisken (643–623 B.C.) and Aspelta (600–580 B.C.); from Nuri; silver, gold, alabaster (calcite), carnelian, turquoise, and steatite; spouted milk vessel: h. 16.4 cm, w. 17.3 cm; alabastron: h. 25.2 cm, diam. 7.2 cm; ewer with handle: h. 31.5 cm; cylinder sheaths: h. 11.3 cm and 12.6 cm, diam. 3.1 cm and 3 cm; tweezers: l. 18 cm, w. 4.3 cm; vessel lid with braided chain: h. 2.8 cm, diam. 8.5 cm; l. of chain: 22 cm; Museum Expedition 20.334, 20.341–342, 20.1070, 21.339–40, 24.901.

Fig. 26. Mask of Queen Malakaye (early sixth century B.C.); from Nuri; gold; h. 13 cm, w. 11.3 cm; Museum Expedition 20.1059.

Fig. 27. A goddess suckling a Nubian queen; from a silver plaque found in the tomb of Nefrukakashta, wife of King Piye, at el Kurru; h. 5.1 cm, w. 1.8 cm, thickness 2 cm; Museum Expedition 24.928; drawing by Nicholas Thayer and Peter Der Manuelian.

Fig. 28. Queen Amanitore smiting enemies; from the pylon of the Lion Temple at Naga; early first century A.D.; from K. Lepsius, *Denkmaeler aus Aegypten und Aethiopien…* (Berlin: Nicolaische Buchhandlung, 1842–45), Abt. 5, pl. 56.

Fig. 29. Queen Amanitore and King Natakamani before the lion-god Apedemak; from the rear wall of the Lion Temple at Naga; from

K. Lepsius, *Denkmaeler aus Aegypten und Aethiopien...* (Berlin: Nicolaische Buchhandlung, 1842–45), Abt. 5, pls. 59–60.

Fig. 30. The upper Deffufa at Kerma (about 1600 B.C.); photograph by Timothy Kendall.

Fig. 31. Mythical beast bed inlays (about 1600 B.C.); from Kerma; ivory; Taweret: h. about 14.5 cm; winged giraffe: h. about 8.5 cm, w. about 9 cm; Museum Expedition 13–12–813, 13–12—817, 13–12–802.

Fig. 32. Ram-head earring (sixth century B.C.); from Meroe; gold; h. 2.9 cm, w. 1.6 cm, d. 1.3 cm; Museum Expedition 23.333.

Fig. 33. Amun as a ram-headed deity inside the mountain at Jebel Barkal; relief carving in temple B 300 (reign of King Taharka, 690–664 B.C); drawing by Timothy Kendall.

Fig. 34. Temple of Ramesses II at Abu Simbel (1279–1212 B.C.); photograph by Torgny Säve-Söderbergh.

Fig. 35. Jebel Barkal with computer reconstruction of the ancient temples; reconstruction and photograph courtesy William Riseman.

Fig. 36. View of the pinnacle and ancient ruins of Jebel Barkal; photograph by Timothy Kendall.

Fig. 37. Winged Isis pectoral (late sixth century B.C.); from Nuri, pyramid of Amaninatakilebte; gold; h. 6.9 cm, w. 16.7 cm; Museum Expedition 20.276.

Fig. 38. Relief of King Thutmose II, Dynasty 18 (1518–1504 B.C.) before the god Dedun; from Semna; sandstone; h. 1.055 m; Museum Expedition 25.1511.

Fig. 39. Detail of the lion-god Apedemak; from inside the west wall of the Lion Temple at Musawarat es-Sufra (late third century B.C.); from F. Hintze, *Musawwarat es-Sufra* I, 2, *Der Löwentempel*, Tafelband (Berlin: Akademie-Verlag, 1971), pls. 71, 73.

Fig. 40. Pottery sherds (6000 B.C.) of the Khartoum Mesolithic; from Kaderu (the Sudan); courtesy of the Peabody Museum of Archaeology and Ethnology, Harvard University.

Fig. 41. Miniature dagger (1700 B.C.); from Kerma; bronze with gold hilt; l. 16.7 cm; Museum Expedition 15–3–421.

Fig. 42. Ram skulls with horn protectors; from Kerma, tombs 1064 and 1042; photographed on March 30, 1913 (expedition negative B 1809).

Fig. 43. Inlays of animal and bird images from a cap (1700 B.C.); from Kerma; mica; bustards: h. 7 cm, w. 8 cm; petals: h. 5.5 cm, w. 1.5–1.8 cm; bands on the border: l. 10.6 cm, w. 2.3 cm; Museum Expedition 13.4284.

Fig. 44. Nineteenth-century view of the pyramids of Meroe; from K. Lepsius, *Denkmaeler aus Aegypten und Aethiopien...* (Berlin: Nicolaische Buchhandlung, 1842–45), Abt. 1, pl. 138.

Fig. 45. Reconstruction of a ba bird statue, Cairo CG 40232; from C. Leonard Woolley and D. Randall-MacIver, *Karanog: The Romano-Nubian Cemetery* 4 (Philadelphia: University Museum, 1910), pls. 1–2. Photograph courtesy of the University Museum, University of Pennsylvania.

Fig. 46. Pastoral scene engraved on a late Meroitic bronze bowl from Karanog; from C. Leonard Woolley and D. Randall-MacIver, *Karanog: The Romano-Nubian Cemetery* 4 (Philadelphia: University Museum, 1910), pls. 26–27.

Fig. 47. Wall painting from the Theban tomb of Rekhmire, vizier under King Thutmose III, Dynasty 18 (1504–1450 B.C.), showing a procession of Nubians with imported goods; from N. de G. Davies, *The Tomb of Rekh-mi-Re at Thebes* (New York: the Metropolitan Museum of Art, 1943), pl. 19.

Fig. 48. The Meroitic alphabet; drawing by Peter Der Manuelian, adapted from the Brooklyn Museum, *Africa in Antiquity* (Brooklyn: Brooklyn Museum, 1978), p. 93, fig. 67.

Fig. 49. Hinged Meroitic bracelet (first century B.C.); from Jebel Barkal; gold and enamel; h. 4 cm, diam. 6 cm; Museum Expedition 20.333.

Fig. 50. Ball pendant, with Hathor head; from el Kurru, pyramid 55 of an unknown queen (mid-eighth century B.C.); rock crystal and gold; h. 5.3 cm, diam. 3.2 cm; Museum Expedition 21.321.

Fig. 51. Modern reproduction of an ancient bed from Kerma; original: 1750–1550 B.C.; wood, rawhide lacing; h. 66 cm, l. 183 cm, w. 73.5 cm; reconstruction by Joseph M. Gerte, Boston; Director's Contingent Fund 40.469.

Fig. 52. Modern-day Nubian bed (1984) in the suk, or market, at Kareima; photograph by Timothy Kendall.

Fig. 53. Assemblage of vessels (1700–1550 B.C.); from Kerma; ceramic; spouted beaker: h. 12 cm; rilled beaker: h. 22.5 cm, diam.: 12.3 cm; miniature beaker: h. 5.5 cm, diam. 6.8 cm; beaker: h. 11 cm, diam. 13 cm; bowl with incised decoration: h. 8 cm, diam. 12.8 cm; bowl: h. 9.2 cm, diam. 10.5 cm; pot with ram's head: h. 22 cm; polished bottle: h. 18.4 cm, diam. 11 cm; Museum Expedition 13.4101, 20.2006, 13.4076, 13–12–936, 13.4105, 16–4–1523, 20.1714, 14–2– 714.

Fig. 54. Meroitic painted pot with crocodiles and vines (second century A.D.); from Kerma; ceramic; diam. 28 cm; Museum Expedition 13.4038.

Fig. 55. Wall painting from the Theban tomb of Rekhmire, vizier under King Thutmose III, Dynasty 18 (1504–1450 B.C.), showing ancient baskets and other goods; from N. M. Davies, *Ancient Egyptian Paintings* I (Chicago, Oriental Institute, University of Chicago, 1936), pl. 16.

Fig. 56. Modern-day baskets for sale in the suk at Aswan; photograph by Paul Tomassetti.

Fig. 57. Female mummy of Queen Nedjmet, Cairo CG 61087, with braided hairstyle; Dynasty 21 (1070–946 B.C.); G. E. Smith, *The Royal Mummies* (Cairo: Imprimerie de l'Institut français d'archéologie orientale, 1912), pl. 69.

Fig. 58. Contemporary Sudanese girl with braided hairstyle; photograph by Timothy Kendall.

Fig. 59. Ancient Nubian relief with tattoos (scarification); from Ursula Hintze, *Meroitica* 5 (1979), p. 139, fig. 8.

Fig. 60. Contemporary Sudanese girl with scarification; photograph by Timothy Kendall.

Fig. 61. Wall relief from the temple of Ramesses III (1194–1163 B.C.) at Medinet Habu, Thebes, showing Nubian wrestlers; from the Epigraphic Survey, *Medinet Habu* II, *Later Historical Records of Ramses III* (Chicago: Oriental Institute, University of Chicago, 1932), pl. 111.

Back cover: statue of King Senkamenisken (643–623 B.C.); from Jebel Barkal; granite; h. 1.47 m; Museum Expedition 23.731.